HOW TO
OPTIONS TRADE

Only after understanding the fundamentals of
trading will you be able to profit from it and with this
manual everything will seem less complicated

ANDREW RAY BUFFET

Contents

INTRODUCTION

Nearly everyone else is afraid to invest in the stock market. And since Options trading is part of the stock market, they're not bothering to learn about it. Some of them assume that investing on the stock market is a dynamic process that requires urgent solutions to make big money. While the others believe it is pure luck, people lose money most of the time.

Most people hesitate to invest in the stock market as they see other people losing money around them. Not to mention that the people who lose money know barely what kind of stocks they buy and how they should control the risks and take advantage of their position.

But the truth is, once you cover the basics of Options trading, you'll learn how to control various assets—stocks, bonds, or other commodities. You see, you get a contract option in Options Trading. And within that contract's time frame, you've got the 'option' to buy, sell, and hand over, or just hold on to, the rights. This resource management gives you infinite opportunities that can ultimately lead to more money. And that's the underlying reason why smart investors choose to trade instead of acquiring the underlying stock in Options Trading. And it goes without saying that buying an options contract is much cheaper than the actual stock, bond or commodity. On top of that, a number of shares can be controlled at a lower price.

Now that you have a good introduction to the world of options trading, let's get you into the doors of the Behind the Scenes so that you can learn how to use everything to earn more.

First of all, you must learn the difference between stocks and options and how they are related. You'll also know the words used in trading options. Next you're going to be armed with different strategies you can choose from time to time to maximize your position, as well as some do's and don'ts you can keep in mind when trading options.

These are the basics. And I would suggest that you start with the practice of trading options in fake environments (there are websites that allow you to practice this without risking real money). Or you can take on the real world of choices if you feel brave enough.

CHAPTER 1

WHAT OPTIONS ARE & HOW THEY WORK

WHAT ARE OPTIONS

Thanks to their simplicity, options are a popular means of trading in the stock market. But this of course means the investor should know their risk appetite to make sure they don't lose more money than they can afford. The explanation why it is appealing to most investors is because when the market index changes, it gives the consumer the power to control their position.

In layman terms, an option is a contract that at a specific date the purchaser has the right to purchase (the right to buy or sell) the underlying asset at a fixed cost. What this means is that you are predetermining the stock price that you want to pay irrespective of the volatility that exist in the contract period. Commonly, a contract option is equal to a company's 100 stocks. The attractive part about the contract options is that it binds the buyer and seller to a contract with strict properties and conditions to reduce the risk of loss.

Consider that sometime later, for example, you want to buy McDonald's stocks (NYSE MCD). The stock's current price is $101 per share. And they're doing pretty well, judging by their current situation, and it's predicted that stock prices could go up in the near future. So, you want to have an option to call (it's a form of contract options that will be discussed later in this book), and you get the right to buy McDonald's stock at $101. I decide to buy 10 stocks in precisely 60 days from now at $101 per share. You should wait now that you have the contract.

Speed forward to 55 days and you see a spike in stock price. Now, that's $200 per unit. But because you had an option contract to buy 10 McDonald stock shares at $101 each, you were able to get it at a deal! That's the best possible scenario. Consider a situation in which the price drops.

Note that McDonald's shares are down to $50 per share instead of rising prices. In this case, if the current price was $50 per share, my options contract would mean a loss for you, and in no way will you buy stocks at $101. You let the contract options expire in this case and instead buy the shares at $50 per share. And that's what it is. That's all. The truth is that without even knowing, you have been dealing for a long time. Think about the time you purchased insurance for your car. It's close to trading options.

When you bought your car, insurance came with it, just in case something happens. You didn't know how much the repairs would cost during that time, nor did you know the car's price as time goes on. Of course, the price may rise, but the insurance will help to protect yourself, just in case. Options trading is almost the same. It's a way to give you the ability to buy a stock at a predetermined rate, and if the price doesn't rise as you like, then you can let the contract expire and then buy the stock in that business.

OPTION CHARACTERISTICS

Before discussing options in depth, let's take a closer look at why you might want to be involved. Did you know that thousands of years ago options were created? Moreover, before the first stock market was established, they were already famous? You may also be surprised to learn that, from conservative, risk-averse buyers to speculators, options can be included in the portfolio of anyone. Due to their flexibility and low cost, many traders love trading options. You can find a way to use options — for income, insurance, hedging, or speculation, no matter what your reason.

INCOME

Options can be used to generate income or cash flow very easily. Basically, you are trading options on stocks that you already own instead of buying shares. You rent your stocks to other people (option buyers) in a way, and they are paying you for the privilege. This can be a profitable way to use an annuity-like product where you can receive cash per month just to keep the stocks.

PROTECTION

Protecting or insuring your savings is another successful use of options. Let's say in one stock you've got a pretty big position. You can use options to protect your stock position in the event of a disaster if you prefer to reduce your risk. And you just hope you don't have to use it like an insurance policy. Options were originally created for this purpose alone. One of the more traditional ways to use the options market is to use options to hedge the stocks.

HEDGING

You will hedge against risk, equivalent to buying stock insurance. Let's presume you're afraid the next year's economy could plunge and take a bite from your portfolio and mutual fund gains. Through holding exchange- traded funds (ETFs) futures that track global indices such as the S&P 500, Dow Jones Industrial Average, Nasdaq-100, or Russell 2000, you will hedge your entire portfolio. Your shares are gaining interest as the market goes down. The pros use options to hedge their stock portfolios on a regular basis, and you can do that too.

SPECULATION

Options have a reputation as a "get-rich-quick" casino because there is so much media attention from speculators. You will maximize your savings with the opportunity to make several times more than you pay for very little upfront money. You are buying many stock shares for a little bit of money with this approach. The best part of these tactics for options is that you always know how much you might risk in advance.

The value in trading options is that in any market environment, you can make money. You may build plans for options that try to take advantage of a demand for bulls, bears, or sideways.

WHAT ARE STOCKS

You are already acquainted with stocks if you're thinking of delving into the realm of options. But just like a refresher, a stock is a piece of a business. When a company decides to be a "public" company, it will issue stock shares for purchase by the general public. The more "stocks" or pieces you buy, the more control you have in the company, the smaller your piece is, unless you own thousands of shares your control or piece is very small.

Now that you are legally a company's co-owner, a part of the earnings are awarded to you. If the business does its best, the stock will rise in value and you will see a profit, generally paid to you in the form of dividends, which are daily (typically quarterly) sums of money paid out to investors. However, if, for one cause or another, the company does not do well, you expect a loss. In this case, the dividends you earn are smaller or you don't get any at all in some cases.

You don't need to own stock in the company you are dealing with in order to trade options. If you are the option's writer/seller, however, owning the stock will reduce your risk.

WHY SHOULD YOU LEARN OPTIONS

Remember what was said by Warren Buffet—never depend on a single source of revenue. And you can diversify your wealth and your overall investment portfolio with the aid of options trading.

This may surprise you, but options are being used as a hedging strategy by large corporations around the world to protect themselves from the risk of losing a lot of money when stock prices suddenly start fluctuating heavily. A great example is the volatility in Forex. When you work in a large corporation, if you are one of their best employees, you may even be offered an options contract.

To cut the chase, trading options gives you the leverage in the trading world and also allows you to get a bigger payout when you decide to sell the stock.

Risk management is the best part of it. If you're a new investor, you should care less about spoiling your investments because it can only look better with trading options.

OPTIONS IN THE STOCK MARKET

While option contracts have existed in some way since the days of ancient Greece, it wasn't until 1973 that the Chicago Board Options Exchange (CBOE) officially institutionalized the exchange of stock options. The general public was highly suspicious of trading stock options prior to the CBOE. Contracts were hard to enforce, and pricing options even had a difficult time for brokers. The CBOE guaranteed that all stock option contracts were structured and that a clearing company (Options Clearing Company or OCC) was established to guarantee the compliance of contracts. There was still a lot of doubt as to whether trading options would catch up with the general public, but the CBOE was buzzing with trading activity after a few years in business. Since that moment, trading options has become an integral facet of major worldwide stock markets.

A total of six options are currently being exchanged in the United States. We all have outstanding platforms where new and experienced traders can gather general information about trading options as well as more specific information about their listings. Such places are good tools and should be looked at as you start the journey of your choices.

American Stock Exchange (AMEX) Boston Options Exchange (BOX)

Chicago Board Options Exchange (CBOE) International Securities Exchange (ISE) New York Stock Exchange (NYSE/ARCA) Philadelphia Stock Exchange (PHLX)

Currently, the options trading system seems to be difficult right off the bat with six markets. Some key players in your trading company stocks, however, will help you navigate these markets and better understand the whole process.

THE BROKER

If you already have a stock broker, he will likely be able to handle trading options for you as well. Many dealers, however, deal specifically with options. As with stocks, you're just asking them what kind of deal you'd like to do, and they're doing the legwork and paying you with a fee to launch the exchange. You can ask them to buy new contracts, sell already- owned contracts, or write new contracts for sale. You can also supply them with some buying and sale orders at different rates. They can manage all aspects of your portfolio of options in general.

Looking for a full-service broker instead of a discount broker as you enter the world of options trading. Only the latter takes orders and carries them out. The former is more expensive, but should take the time to visit you personally and get to know your financial circumstances and investment goals.

When you believe that you are experienced dealing with options and have become very hands-on in your trading, you may want to go with a discount broker which is a less expensive option.

THE MARKET MAKER

The market maker is not a person you're ever going to meet or see. Actually, the term refers to a broker-dealer business that bears the burden of holding multiple shares of a given security in order to be able to trade in that security. In other words, as the name suggests, the market maker does – offers a demand for your options order. They are there to keep the markets running smoothly and to provide some stability. To do this, by maintaining a large and varied portfolio of contract options, they step in if there are no government orders to meet a necessary deal.

For example, suppose you want to buy options contracts for Google, but no one is currently selling from the general public. The market maker steps in from his own portfolio and sells you those options.

If not for market makers, sales would exist far less, it could be difficult to buy or sell, and the options available would be severely restricted.

THE OPTIONS CLEARING CORPORATION

The Options Clearing Corporation (OCC) is the agency that guarantees that sellers' options meet their obligations and complete their transactions. It essentially transfers billions of dollars a day as a clearing house, making it one of the world's largest equity derivatives clearing organizations. You're not going to have to call them, most likely, but it's good to know that they're there to make business run smoothly.

OPTIONS INDUSTRY COUNCIL

This is an investing education collaboration established by the above- mentioned six options exchanges. The OIC is a wonderful tool for those new to the options market, and its website provides a wealth of information on the stock options listed.

WHY WERE OPTIONS SUCH A HIT?

As you can see, in the last few decades, Options trading has gained a lot of attention. For its resounding success, there is no definitive explanation. Just like any other brand or endeavor, before testing the market, there was no way to be sure of that popularity. Part of the options trading appeal, no doubt, is the potential to make money faster and bigger than in the traditional stock market. Options also provide an incentive for investors to compete with less exposure in the stock market. That's because you don't have to buy stock shares for stock-related trading options. If an investor is familiar with a certain stock and assumes that it can anticipate its progress, then purchasing an option gives the investor an ability to capitalize on the action of that stock without having to buy the stock directly.

OPTIONS VS. STOCKS

Not everyone interested in trading options is "playing" the stock market. Because of the threat, your broker can recommend against it, based on your financial portfolio and your priorities. So it depends on how eager you are to take a chance with your money whether or not you get involved.

In reality, the stock market is easier to navigate than the options market. Generally speaking, you have only one thing to worry about—whether the stock goes up or down. You have to get three things right for choices, the way it's going, the pacing, and the size. Losses tend to be smaller in stock transactions—you rarely lose 100% of your investment as with options. Therefore, if a stock is in a state of deficit, you should typically only wait for it to return to fair market value.

Methods can be intimidating, but they have their advantages. Investing in options helps you to tie up much less of the cash on hand. Therefore, the leveraging power of options is greater. There is definitely also the opportunity for higher returns, particularly with less cash outlay. Finally, options are a very dynamic investment tool that generate more alternative investments, suitable for those who want a diverse portfolio. In reality, there is no guarantee for either stocks or options. Together with your agent, it's your job to determine what kind of chances you can take and whether you can deal with the potential consequences. That's why books like this are essential, outlining the fundamentals and explaining the strategies.

WHY TRADE OPTIONS

This is a common question that people ask. Why are you going to trade options? Okay, the first explanation is to cover the risk and to control it. If you take a huge risk, Options trading is the way to protect yourself so you don't lose all your money. It gives you full control over how the money goes and where it goes.

Yet one thing you should consider is that with closed eyes, options should not be sold. You're going to have to watch the competition constantly. And if you don't, it will backfire.

HEDGING AND SPECULATION

Hedging and speculation are the first two things to learn before investing a single penny in trading options. That's what's going to get you started and how to treat options trading.

Hedging is when you feel that something might go wrong. It doesn't mean that something will necessarily go wrong, if things start to go bad, it's just a way to protect yourself (i.e., your money).

Hedging is the way to secure your savings in the event of a fall in prices. Hedging, in other words, is your shield against a lot of money being wasted. Hedging is used to cover themselves by both large corporations and retail investors.

On the other hand, if you have no understanding of the underlying asset (stock, debt or commodity) while using options as a hedging tool, you will surely lose money according to experts. That's because you're trying to gamble too much and buy insurance on something you don't care about. This means that rather than taking a risk and increasing your profits, you will be losing money in the insurance. Hedging, however, is a great way to protect yourself against failures if done correctly. Speculation is next. But it's pretty risky.

Each shareholder makes profit in three ways—when the price goes up, when the price goes down, and when the price changes sideways (meaning the price remains or goes up and down within a range). Speculation will make a lot of money.

Speculation can be done by market analysis and review. It includes assessing and forecasting patterns and working out from the current point where the market is going to go. If you are familiar with the market and have deep knowledge of the underlying asset, this can be a huge advantage.

Speculation, though, as I said earlier, is quite dangerous. A shareholder who wishes to benefit as a speculator must be able to determine accurately the trajectory of the asset price (whether it will go up or down), the timing of that direction and the extent (the price will change by how much).

ADVANTAGES AND DISADVANTAGES OF OPTIONS TRADING

We accept that Options trading is difficult. But once you grasp it, it becomes an ability you recognize easily. The best part about options trading is that without actually investing in the asset, you can profit from the price movement of the underlying asset.

And as I mentioned earlier, investing in options is actually cheaper than investing in the real asset. And, if you invest directly in the property, you'd have less leverage. In short, you potentially have access to much more assets than you would previously have through options trading.

And if you add up everything, the assets, capital, etc., you'll find that an investor will actually earn more money per real dollar invested relative to investing directly in the asset. An investor can also lose only a set amount of money with options, which is essentially the premium he/she has paid.

This means you're not going to lose anything if you don't put everything in the premium. This is the best thing to do if you just want to test the waters and you're not able to go into it.

Another great advantage of Options Trading is that you can use hedging to cover yourself from risks becoming too high as an insurance policy. This means you can also protect yourself against heavy stock market fluctuations. I would highly recommend that you consider hedging to reduce the risks as much as possible.

Another advantage is that even if the stock doesn't make money, you can make money. This is due to the free trade to increase your leverage and profits, down or sideways. Several times, you'll see the stock price drop, and by the end of it, you can still make a profit.

However, the fees are much less for trading options (now you know why stock brokers are warning you against it). And if you choose to go through an online broker, because they want to beat their competition, these commissions are even lower.

In contrast, Options trading is flexible. It allows you to react according to the location of the price. It also gives you the opportunity to participate in more than one business. This means that from food to foreign currency, you can invest in anything. And, with big corporations, you don't have to spend a huge amount of money. All you need is a minimum amount and you can begin to make money.

Last but not least, and this one is a biggie, the rate at which the profit comes in. Yes, you get your profit as soon as the stock rises so you can start investing in other markets or stocks. The acceleration of the economy allows you to compete concurrently in more markets and therefore earn more money.

So compared to other forms of day trading, options trading is only a short-term investment. It means that you will lose money within a few months, even if you make an inaccurate predication, instead of waiting for years to lose money due to that error.

Taxes are a drawback when it comes to trading options. Indeed, except for some rare circumstances, you're going to have to pay taxes on everything you do. And make sure you fill out your IRA form before you start investing and make sure you keep track on taxes.

In addition, unlike shares, when it comes to options, there is no deposit certificate. It's just paying rights, so it doesn't give you a proof of ownership. This means that unless it is a stock certificate, you will not be able to prove ownership of the stocks to people.

And then there's the uncertainty problem. If you participate in something you don't know about, it's a bit scary. That's why most investors make sure they have in-depth, accurate knowledge of the stuff they invest in because it can easily turn into a gamble not worth the profits.

Knowing your strategy is important. And be sure to start slow so small in order not to lose large. It's like driving a car. When you're driving for the first time, everything is scary. Yet you learn the tricks of the trade as you spend more and more time behind the wheel and instantly you become the best driver.

CHAPTER 2

TRADING FUNDAMENTALS

Patience is indeed a quality for the reader who is completely new to the world of options trading, when you negotiate the often confusing world of stock options. Keep the confidence that you will eventually develop an understanding of how options work and how the various types of choices and tactics come into play. This book makes it as simple as you can.

Trading options may seem difficult at a glance, but when you understand some of the basic concepts and terminology involved, it's really not so bad. You may have to re-read some parts of this book over and over and over again and have to resort to some pencil-and-paper equations to work it all out, but with some training and some "digital" trading, you may finally feel confident enough to give it a shot.

This section offers you the real nuts-and-bolts and discusses the two main types of trading options: the put option and the call option.

CALLS & PUTS—WHAT'S IN A NAME ?

The call option may be the best form of alternative to understand. It's called a call because at any point before the expiration date, the buyer/owner will "call" to sell the stock. The person who sells the order, also known as the writer of the call, decides at any point before the expiry date to sell the stock (underlying asset) at the agreed-upon value.

A shareholder would choose to purchase a call because they expect that over a given period of time the underlying asset will see a price increase. Calls have an expiry date and the asset can be acquired at any point before or on that day.

It is essential to have expiration dates. The inventory in question must behave in a certain manner (it must either go up or down) within a certain period of time in order for the buyer / owner of an option to benefit from it. The higher the period of time before expiry, the greater statistical probability the stock would behave in the desired manner. Hence — time is money— the most important principle of options trading. The more time between the point at which the option is acquired and the point at which the option expires in an option agreement, the more beneficial the offer will be.

A call option's opposite is a put option, and a put option has a buyer/owner and a seller/writer, like the call option. A put option is so named because the investor is entitled to sell his stock to the market at any point within an agreed-upon time frame at an agreed-upon value. The author of a put option actually agrees to buy the stock at any point within the agreed-upon time frame at the agreed-upon price. If they expected the underlying asset to fall in price, an investor would buy a put option. So you've got it, the fundamentals of trading options. There are literally countless possibilities and prospects for successful trade from these fundamental concepts. Let's build your understanding of options trading dynamics by walking over a few specific examples of each trading form.

OPTION VARIANTS

There are options contracts for long-term shareholders that can be held for many years. This is very similar to traditional investing on the stock market where an investor trades directly in the underlying asset. A simple option is a simple put or call option. While it may be a simple option, an exotic alternative, or a completely different option.

TRANSACTING OR CLOSING OUT AN OPTION TRADE

The truth is that most options are not acquired or sold before the contract expiry date. Clearly, most investors are not exercising their rights. The right owners often auction off their choice deals, while some writers buy back or have their own rights. About 60% of the options are either sold or phased out, while 30% are exhausted and become useless. Currently, only 10% of all options are exercised. And that's all right because there are occasions when the price of the opportunity itself can prove to be lucrative enough for you to trade away.

HOW OPTIONS ARE PRICED

Options are priced depending on the "premium." The option's premium is simply the option's intrinsic value, plus a time value depending on length. Comparing it to an insurance premium, which is what you pay for the option, is the best way to understand it. For trading options, that's what you pay for the right you're going to buy and the stock you're going to get.

OPTIONS AND LEVERAGING EXAMPLE:

Consider that a shareholder bought 100 shares of a single institutional stock at $100 each, which cost him $10,000 each. He also has five $200 premium call options with a $100/share strike price in addition to just the stock, which will allow him to buy 500 shares as well.

Let's assume that after a month, the share price rose to $110. This would translate to a profit of $1,000. What if for each deal the option premium for the same stock always rises to $300?

The gain is 10 percent for regular stock investment; the gain is 50 percent for its stock option prices.

But by buying 500 more stocks at $50,000 and selling them at $55,000, if he wants to use all five options. That would have made him a profit of $5,000.

But again, exploiting also has drawbacks. The dollar loss is magnified if the market has not risen in the right direction.

If the share price falls to $80 ($10 less than the strike price of the option) using the same scenario, the loss will be 20 percent. On the other hand, the premium option could be lowered to $80, resulting in a total loss of 60 percent.

That's why investors need to use their discretion wisely when trading options. Before investing in it, they should also have a good market forecast. They should also continually look at the company in which we spend and see how their earnings are being made.

TIME FRAME

There is no expiration date for a standard stock. What this means is that the stockholder will hold on forever to his stocks. On the other hand, there is a fixed expiration date for stock options. And an option will only become null if it is not exercised before the expiry date.

OWNERSHIP

Ownership of a share of the stock is indicated by a company-issued certificate. But, a stock option does not have an ownership stamp. It's just a bond, and it's owned by anyone who holds it. There are no documents, but, for choices, you just get the option.

VOLUME

A company may issue only a set number of shares. Consequently, buyers can exchange only a small number of shares. On the other hand, there is no cap as to the amount of stock options that buyers will buy or sell for. Nevertheless, if the option is not exercised, a stock option will not offer dividends, voting rights, or control of the company.

MARKET EXCHANGES

Trading options for professional traders, individual investors and companies is available on the options exchange. A variety of options contracts can be transacted at the same time by an individual.

Unlike standard securities, on a SEC-regulated market, a stock option is exchanged. Brokers and daily stocks promote trades in options. It is easy to monitor purchases and results across their respective marketplaces.

SOME IMPORTANT TERMS

STRIKE PRICE

The strike price is the value of the underlying asset that can be sold or acquired when the right is exercised by an investor. It impacts the option's viability, and when it comes to how much it will go for, it is the main determining factor in the option's price.

It implies that if the underlying asset is a bid and if it is a call option, in order to generate a profit, the stock price must be higher than the strike price. If it is a put option, in order to create value, the stock price has to be cheaper than the strike price. The right cannot be exercised unless the conditions are met before the contract expires. A listed option is traded on an exchange of options such as the Options Exchange CBOE or Chicago Board. It has a fixed date of expiry and price of hit.

LISTED OPTION

An option listed is equal to 100 stock shares. If the current market price of the underlying asset itself is higher than the strike price, a call option is "in - the-money" (meaning it is profitable).

On the other hand, if the asset's price is lower than the strike price, a put option is "in - the-money." The intrinsic value is the quantity by which the in - the-money alternative is.

1. PREMIUM

The premium is the option's overall price. Factors that affect the premium include inflation, time value, strike price, and the underlying asset's size. Calculating the premium alternative is usually difficult, but not with a good pricing model to follow (more on a later chapter on this). The premium, however, is often the intrinsic of the asset, plus the time value.

It is simply the price that the buyer option needs to pay when they select the option seller. It's the risk associated with it, and it can be a small or a big amount. It is also dictated by the market's price, and if the stock has a higher risk, the premium will grow. This is equivalent to insurance, because if there is a higher risk as a result of injuries or having had many medical problems, the premium would rise as a result.

The intrinsic value, if it is a call option, is known as the' in - the-money number'-or the strike price. On the other hand, the time value is likely to raise the option's interest. If the price is $9.25, for example, the intrinsic value may be $9 while the time value is $0.25. In most cases, more than their intrinsic value, options are sold.

2. CONVERSION

When a call option is offered, a position option is acquired, or at least 2 options have the same expiry and strike price, a transfer is made. Compared to existing stock, it is usually done when the options are overpriced. As a consequence, doing this helps you to make a risk-free income, and if you see something like this, then you take advantage of it.

A delta is the price change of an option while an exercise is a decision to trade the choice generated by the right in the deal. This is widely used when there is a difference in the economy and prices change. An expiry is the date of end of the contract. Which means the right is not valid anymore and is gone. The grantor is an organization or person who is willing to exercise the right before the contract expires. The stock option expires on the expiry month's third Friday.

INTRINSIC VALUE

The intrinsic value is the option's price when exercised immediately. If it has no intrinsic value, an option is said to be out-of-the-money.

A strangle is a position involving the purchase of both call and place options with different strike prices but similar expiry. The time value is a premium component beyond the intrinsic value.

UNDERLYING ASSET

An underlying asset is an option seller's form of security. It is an obligation to offer in case the right is exercised to buy from the option holder. In this case, this is some of the stock in a particular company. For currencies, indexes, and commodities, these options are usually also open.

Those basic terms are what you need to learn when dealing with stock market options. Understanding these basic conditions should place you on the right path to success.

An underlying asset is an option seller's form of security. It is an obligation to offer in case the right is exercised to buy from the option holder. In this case, this is some of the stock in a particular company. For currencies, indexes, and commodities, these options are usually also open.

An underlying asset is an option seller's form of security. It is an obligation to offer in case the right is exercised to buy from the option holder. In this case, this is some of the stock in a particular company. For currencies, indexes, and commodities, these options are usually also open.

An underlying asset is an option seller's form of security. It is an obligation to offer in case the right is exercised to buy from the option holder. In this case, this is some of the stock in a particular company. For currencies, indexesy also open.

CHAPTER 3

OPTIONS PRICING & OPTIONS TRADING PLATFORMS

Most people find trading options hard to understand. This is mainly because all of its pieces are hard to understand. However, once people understand the science behind trading options, they will potentially leverage their art form to achieve their investment goals. The price of an option depends heavily on the price of the underlying asset, the value of the asset, and the available period before the contract expires. This chapter will explain how the price and exchange option works, and at the center what it entails.

THE ASSET'S PRICE

At the heart, the underlying asset's price is critical when pricing options. It's what all is based on, and it's the asset's worth. It's what's going to also decide the options for putting and calling, and it's what you're going to look into spending in.

Essentially, when the price of the commodity decreases, the price of the call option always increases. The prices of the put option, however, are dropping.

If the asset price drops, on the other hand, the opposite happens. The price of the put option is increasing and the price of the call option is that. This is to ensure that the choices for putting and calling suit whatever it does. If the commodity is only relevant for a short period of time, a put option is widely used by people. But if the commodity has value, you can also place a call option on it.

Prior to the expiry of options, time is important for pricing options. The longer the date of maturity, the higher the price of the contract. The price choice declines as time moves towards expiry. That's why it's important to see the immediate gains from it, because the price of an option may decline over time, and you may not ever get the stock again for that price.

VOLATILITY

Volatility is also a factor in option pricing. For stocks, the stable ones have lower option premiums than the extremely volatile options. There is also something called implied volatility, based on the market maker's confidence. If a lot of people invest in a particular stock, it will raise its price. To can the premium option, the market maker should change the implied volatility.

An option is a cheaper alternative to a stock as a flexible purchase. Trading options will produce more profits by exploiting. It also limits the risk as a whole. You're not going to put all your resources into one thing, hoping it's not going to fall. However, as an option is only available until the expiry date, the capital will not always be stuck in it.

Only up to the option premium can an owner lose money- essentially what they first paid for the option. In addition to the fee, which could be a small price to pay in the case of a stock, they won't lose anything else unless there is a bid on it. Margin conditions are therefore not necessary if an alternative is to be acquired by the buyer.

On the other hand, if the buyer has exercised his right, the option writer will buy or sell the underlying asset. A writer of options will retain the bonus money paid by the option holder- but only if the buyer failed to buy or sell the underlying asset before the contract expires. As such, the writer's part needs a margin requirement.

THEORETICAL VALUE OF AN OPTION

A theoretical value varies from a premium option. As discussed above, the next option buyer charges an incentive fee so that he/she can buy or sell the underlying asset before the contract right expires.

The theoretical valuation is simply an approximation of the option's present value. It is calculated based on the price model chosen formula. This covers variables such as pre-expiry duration, strike price, and underlying asset quality. The potential interest fluctuates constantly until the option expires due to the changes certain variables experience during the lifespan of the option.

An option pricing model produces a theoretical value. That factor has a certain value and at a future time it is part of the theoretical value. If the stock is selected as the underlying asset, its theoretical value includes implied volatility based on the supply and demand of the option. An investor uses various pricing models to learn the theoretical value of the decision.

The estimate involves factors such as implied volatility, duration, strike price, and underlying asset worth. As these variables always change, a potential value changes over time. This theoretical value is used by many investors and traders to know the value and risk of the option in order to make an intelligent decision. Trading platforms also provide modified prices, while online pricing calculators can also be used.

Before you start, it is important to use a statistical formula to determine how much you can potentially make off of an option or stock. Using this formula will help give you a good idea of what you're going to get out of it, and that's why it will help you decide whether or not it's worth investing in that choice.

You will manipulate the market and get the most for the money you put into it, understanding the fundamentals of how markets operate, the funds, and what happens to them.

OPTIONS PRICING MODELS AND MARKETS

Here are a few pricing models to adopt when attempting to determine the price of an option. You only need to grasp a few good models thoroughly, and then use an online calculator. Each segment will go over some of the basic models and how you can understand them.

THE BLACK-SCHOLES MODEL

In 1973, as a computing option premium, Robert Merton, Myron Scholes, and Fischer Black developed the Black-Scholes pricing model. This model has become the most famous since that period. Indeed, two years after Black died in 1995, Merton and Scholes received a Nobel Prize in Economics. Nevertheless, Black was still remembered for his work, although he was not given the Nobel Prize because only living people are awarded the Nobel Prize.

The Black-Scholes formula applies only to European calls; both call and put, and in its estimation does not include paid dividends. Nevertheless, using the asset's ex-dividend value can still be used.

The model assumes that when it expires, the option can only be exercised. So that's why they're considering only European solutions. In fact, apart from not including paid dividends, no fees are also taken into account in this process.

It also means the economy is productive and market movements are not reliable. Volatility and interest rates that are risk-free are stable and well known. Finally, the Black-Scholes model assumes normal distribution of returns.

This alternative takes only one volatile asset, such as a portfolio, and then a risk-free asset, such as cash, into account. There is no settlement option with this, but with this arrangement there is a way for someone to borrow money at a risk-free basis. With this model, you can buy any stock, even a fraction of it, without any hidden fees or expenses. The options are calculated at the moment with this decision, as well as the payout. With a short investment option, you can create a long stock investment.

The Black-Scholes model requires the following to measure the option value:

- Risk-free interest rate Implied volatility
- Timing (expressed as a percentage of the year) Strike price
- Current asset price

The mathematical formula is complicated. To use it, an average person can be scared. Fortunately, online calculators are available that can be used to measure the price using this pattern. In fact, trading platforms have analytical tools that can be used to determine the price.

This is a good way to get an investing estimate, but it's not the only thing you're going to rely on. It may lead you to subject yourself to some major risks due to market fluctuations, liquidity risks, and sudden changes and threats. There are also drastic fluctuations in prices, and most of the time money in the real world does not come with an unchanging interest. It's a good way to get an idea of what you're about to do, but you shouldn't rely entirely on it at the same time.

THE COX-RUBINSTEIN BINOMIAL OPTION PRICING MODEL

Mark Edward Rubenstein, Stephen Ross, and Carrington Cox created a variant of the Black-Scholes pattern, the Cox-Ross-Rubenstein model. This model's primary advantage is that it uses a lattice-based model and over time takes into account the price movement of the underlying asset. A lattice-based model calculates the option's lifetime shifts in multiple variables. Consequently, the effect is a more accurate price choice. It looks like a tree, and the depletion of the stock is advancing in that direction.

Used for American options, this model. This implies that all are immune to risk so that returns are equal to risk-free interest rate.

The Cox-Ross-Rubenstein model therefore states that because the economy is perfectly efficient, arbitration is not feasible. The underlying asset's price can never go up and down at the same time. At any given time, it can only go in one direction. During the life of the contract, different points in time can be defined. Because of that, a binomial tree can be formed.

It is usually calculated from the start of the option to the end of the option, and then back again. Once this is done, it is then measured along with adjustments in option rates along with the parameters of the increases in dividend prices. All this is collectively calculated and put into a theoretical model to help others understand where their money will go.

The greatest benefit to this is that it works on American stocks. One downside is that it also allows you to see precisely where a stock is at a particular point. You should take a look at this, and you'll learn about where that stock will be in the future through its empirical properties. In this way, it is beneficial.

But the biggest limitation is that calculating takes forever. All at the same time you are analyzing a lot of numbers, and many of the older computers can't do that. However, with the technological changes, algorithms should keep up with the rate of changing numbers. You should get an online calculator to see where a stock is going to be at a certain point in time. Like the Cox-Ross-Rubenstein model, online price calculators and trading site analytical tools can be used to know the price of the contract.

THE PUT/CALL PARITY

Hans Stoll introduced the put/call parity as a pricing concept in 1969. There is a relationship between the European call and place options with similar strike price and expiry date, according to his study.

This implies that there is a specific fixed option value for each call option value at a given strike price. The same applies to the values of the option. There is a matching call option value at a common strike price for a put option value. The relationship exists because a position is generated that is the same as the underlying asset when there is a mixture of alternatives for positioning and calling.

The returns for the underlying asset and right must be identical in order to avoid arbitration. If the opportunity arises, traders and investors who take advantage of arbitration will make a profit.

The parity put/call is used to check EU options pricing models. If the parity test is not satisfied with the result of the pricing model, it means that negotiation will take place and the model must be dismissed as a pricing strategy. There are several methods to measure the parity of the place / call.

Thankfully, certain trading platforms provide tools for analysis. Which offer simulation of the parity of the place/call.

But you don't have to memorize all the pricing models completely, of course. Just choose one that suits your situation, have a handy online pricing model calculator, and let the numbers move for you.

WHAT IS PAPER TRADING

Many new traders are attracted by the various trading markets, some of whom are long-term traders, while others are looking for short-term trading. Common to all new traders is some understandable uncertainty and anxiety about their trading loss of money.

While there are dangers to any form of trading, brokers offer a variety of tools to help first-time traders develop their trading skills. One is called "paper trading," although you're less likely to hear the word, being a term for what's known as show trading. The word ' paper trading' derives from the stock exchange market, where investors will write their assets on paper to track the actions of the market.

ADVANTAGES OF PAPER TRADING

TRADING WITHOUT THE RISK

Demo accounts are commonly used by first-time traders who want to experiment before dealing with real money to know how to deal. Other users of paper trading/demo accounts are more experienced traders who want to test new strategies or practice on new channels of trading, learn about the market and, most importantly, learn about themselves as traders. Needless to say, in the trading world this is a very useful tool.

VIRTUAL ACCOUNT

Using a demo account helps traders to observe and interact with an account that looks similar to the real use of online trading accounts by traders for the first time. Demo account owners in the beginning earn a quantity of virtual money and can start trading by opening positions for sale and buy. The demo account shows market movements on the screens of the traders, just like a real account, so they can determine whether to continue their trading or get out. We should review their activities at the end of the day, learn from them, and get ready to start trading on their real account. It is not only necessary for demo account users to work on demo accounts, but also to look back and learn from their acts. This is also important for more seasoned traders who, for whatever reason, want to train on the demo account. We need to test if their trades are as good as at the end of the day we wished.

DISADVANTAGES OF PAPER TRADING

Nonetheless, there are some risks that should not be overlooked for paper trading. For a number of reasons, certain people would suggest you not to start with a demo account.

EUPHORIA TRADING

According to them, the key one is the feeling it can provide to euphoria paper trading. Since no real money is being used, traders will take risks they would not otherwise take, thus increasing their earnings. On the other hand, a case of money loss is often not taken very seriously because the loss is not real money. There's another drawback; since they're not trading with their money, they're not always going to follow the market and respond as if it were their own money.

DELAYED DATA

Many test accounts do not use up-to-date information directly, but they postpone it by 15-20 minutes, because rivals do not use the details. Some show fake data, but the main objective remains the same—to train traders for the Forex

41

market. Brokers use the device on all forms of markets around the world–Forex, futures, shares, commodities, etc. Because of the fact that no real money is brought in, it is often called "Paper money," "Monopoly money," etc.

WHAT IS SWING TRADING

Swing trading is a trading style that attempts to capture gains in a stock (or any financial instrument) from a few days to a few weeks. Swing traders mainly look for trading opportunities using technical analysis. In addition to studying market trends and patterns, these traders can use fundamental analysis.

UNDERSTANDING SWING TRADING

Swing trading means holding a position for more than one trading session, either long or short, but typically no more than a few weeks or months. This is a general time period, as some transactions may last more than a few months, although the broker may still find swing trades.

Swing trading's aim is to grab a chunk of a possible price change. While some traders with lots of volatility are searching for volatile stocks, others may choose more sedated stocks. Swing trading in either case is the method of determining where the price of an asset is likely to move next, taking a spot, and then gaining a chunk of that move's income.

Successful swing traders are only looking to capture a chunk of the price move predicted, and then move on to the next chance.

Swing trading is one of the most popular forms of active trading where traders use various forms of technical analysis to hunt for intermediate-term opportunities. You should be intimately familiar with technical analysis if you are engaged in swing trading.

On a risk/reward basis, many swing traders evaluate trades. When evaluating an asset map, they decide where they're going to enter, where they're going to put a stop loss, and then predict where they can make a profit. If on a setup that could reasonably yield a gain of $3, they risk $1 per share, that's a favorable risk / reward. On the other hand, it's not as favorable to risk $1 to make $1 or just make $0.75.

Due to the short-term nature of the trades, swing traders primarily use technical analysis. That said, to improve the analysis, conceptual analysis can be used. For instance, if a swing trader sees a bullish setup in a market, they might want to test that the asset's dynamics look favorable or are also improving.

PROS

- takes less selling time than day trading
- maximizes the opportunity for short-term profit by catching the bulk of market swings
- traders may rely exclusively on technical analysis to simplify the trading cycle

CONS

- trading positions are subject to market risk overnight and weekend
- abrupt market reversals may lead to significant losses
- swap traders frequently ignore longer-term patterns in favour of short-term market movements

CHAPTER 4

INVESTING

Now that you're comfortable with the mechanics of buying stock options, it's time to learn how to do that. It may seem like a mad ordeal to buy stock option, but the fact is, it's not. The chapter will discuss how to purchase stock options and what to do when you do it.

Note... Investors need to remember that they only take advantage of the profit potential within a certain time frame when they buy options. They're not getting the product themselves. Often, when kept for a long time, options decrease in value. This means you need to use it as fast as possible when it is available to you.

Note that a call option simply grants the buyer the right to purchase a fixed amount of the underlying asset's securities at the strike price as long as it has not yet expired. A put option, on the other hand, is only a right to sell within a certain period of time a fixed number of the asset's securities at a specified price. It may sound boring, but knowing the difference between the two is crucial for beginners.

Next, an investor must determine the type of underlying asset in which to invest. He / she also has to assess the asset's price

45

path. That's where you should first go. It is important to decide what to invest in. You have to examine the business at hand several times and see the patterns that are made with a stock. If the stock doesn't do well, don't look to invest it. Then, move on to something else that will have a better chance of succeeding.

You should also continue with non-volatile goods. It could go from high to small in a competitive stock within a day or two. It's hard to control these kinds of stocks and it could set you up for failure. Instead, once you spend in it, you have a stock option that is less risky but still has the potential to be lucrative.

CHARTING

Charting tools can be used to draw lines of resistance and help and metrics can be used to assess the asset's price path. There are also various chart templates that help you determine where the price is going to go, and the following pages will explore them more.

BEAR OR BULL SPREAD ?

The next move is to choose either a bull put or a bear call spread based on levels of resistance or assistance. This will decide how the stock option will be distributed and if you choose to invest in it.

A level of resistance or support is a certain price range or cap where it is difficult to reach the price of an item. It's therefore an extraordinary level that an asset can hit. Once the price of a commodity reaches a level of resistance, it typically returns to the original prices. A level of resistance is usually a high price limit, whereas a level of support is usually a low price limit.

Stop losses are also placed below the level of support or above the level of resistance. As the name implies, during your trades, they are designed to' vent losses.'

A variation of the bear call is used with degrees of resistance. This includes calls with the same termination, but it is followed by different strikes. The aim of the bear call spread is to preserve an underlying bearish or neutral position. Upon retiring, this technique relies on a premium's productivity. The variance takes into account that the initial price will fall behind, and the stock will ultimately be lower. In other words, to the peak or dropping, you would EXPECT the price of the commodity. That option requires you already have to pay the outlay to decide where it is going to go. Where it ends up is not fully known at first, but it's a good way to see how the payout is going to be as the stock option begins to fall. The most you get out of this is the premium number, and the most you can lose is the value to be used with support levels until the long-call thresholds are listed at that point, so it's important to be careful when doing a bear-call spread. It's done with a short and a long put, with less than the short being the long. It encourages the buyer to get back some of his capital and is lucrative when the economy begins to move. It has minimal opportunity and risk, and the most that the individual will receive is the premium plus any pattern the market wants to raise. With this, the most you can lose is when the long put is capped, but the probability is smaller most of the time. Nevertheless, with this, it takes a little more of a guess as to where this supply will finally go. If you try to assess where the profit margins will eventually end up going, you will know the figures. The bull put spread's aim is to remain bullish or neutral to the underlying asset. In other words, to the recession or increase you would EXPECT the price of the commodity.

Deciding at what price a spread will be set is critical. In most situations, the price of a distribution of the bear call is above the level of resistance. Nonetheless, the price of the bull put spread is set below the level of support.

POTENTIAL PROFIT/LOSS

It is possible to manually measure the opportunity for profit / loss. Typically, though, a broker offers instruments that investors can use to determine. Therefore, the spread differential times 100 minus the benefit is known as the investor's risk exposure:

Risk Exposure = [(|Sell posn. - Buy Posn.|) x 100] – profit

In order to justify the risk, it is best to ensure that there is adequate profit. It is also possible to use probability calculators to measure the hazard areas and break even points. Investors are encouraged to retain a clear likelihood of success and never neglect it in return for a greater benefit.

The differential can be positioned near the price of the underlying asset between selling and buying positions. Of example, for a bear call spread, the buyer will sell a $140 call option and buy the $141 call option. The investor, on the other hand, can also sell an option of $125 put and buy the option of $124 put for a bull put spread.

$1 price-based losses aren't a big deal-compared to the chance of huge, leveraged profits when prices go the right way.

PRICE MONITORING

Monitoring price movements on a daily basis is critical for the investor. If the underlying asset's price goes in the right direction, the investor in the holding may cause the option to expire. On the contrary, at a loss, the investor can buy back the sold option but retain the option; it can raise value until it even makes a profit or breaks. That's why a lot of people watch the markets like a hawk to decide when a person should buy the opportunity they have, or whether they should wait for the right moment. One day's missing might change everything.

In fact, by selling out whenever he / she makes a profit, the buyer will close the position. If you're making a profit from this, it's best to get out now before the market changes. You can use all your losses as an excuse to get out before you risk all, because as you become more acquainted with what you're doing, you'll realize when it's time to get out and when you're supposed to stay in the warehouse.

MANAGING OPTIONS

HOW TO HOLD & BUY WITH OPTIONS

Buying options do not guarantee that they are exercised by the buyer until expiry. In addition, there are three methods of using choices.

First, the buyer should hold the mature option before it expires and then purchase the underlying asset at the agreed price. Investors do this when the current market price is higher than the strike price if the commodity has risen up.

Second, sometime before it expires, the buyer merely exercises the right. This is achieved when the asset price fluctuates up and down the agreed price. If the investor assumes the price will not go any further, he / she will exercise the option immediately after a higher price than the strike price has been registered.

Finally, the investor can cause the option to expire. Investors do this if the underlying asset's price continues to decline. The loss suffered by buyers is restricted only to the premium option.

HOW TO SELL WITH OPTIONS

Unlike investors, if the holders want to use it, option writers will sell or buy the underlying asset. Within the negotiated contract period, they will buy or sell the asset at the strike price-even if the asset's market price is higher or lower than the agreed price.

A covered call enables the writer/seller to sell his/her own underlying asset. If the customer uses the right, the call writer will sell the commodity at the agreed price. This enables the writer to receive all of the stock's benefits as well as the dividends. The only way this does not happen is when the person decides to share the shares received with the stock.

There's still the problem of the individual who doesn't completely profit from this, however. We have recovered the premium and dividend, but they have stayed out of any other potential market rising, so you should be careful before going into this.

On the other hand, an undisclosed call allows the vendor to sell the commodity he / she does not own at the outset of the deal. If the price of the underlying asset has risen sharply and the investor wants to exercise the option, the seller will lose a lot of money. It means the seller will only have to acquire the asset at a high price to market it to the buyer. As a result of the transaction, this can cause a significant risk, and it can result in the investor losing a lot of money in the purchase.

WATCH THE MARKET

Traders' allowing their options to expire is a common observation. This is true for long-term markets. To make the alternative competitive, the demand must hit a level. If a trader wants to accept an alternative, he/she will evaluate the probability that a certain price will be met by the consumer. No fair deal is assured by a cheap price. A good demand and prospects means it's going to be a good deal.

If you are looking to buy a stock option, you will watch the market for a certain period of time. See the trend and see if there's a chance with that for benefit. If it is, it is time to go for it. If not, it may be best to sit out that one and not take the risk with it. You will watch the market every day by monitoring stocks and seeing which ones are doing well and which ones are going to stay away.

THE AVERAGE MONTHLY RANGE

Most traders prefer to look at the premium option rather than the potential returns. While significant, they tend to focus too much on it, while ignoring the likelihood that the demand may hit and inevitably surpass the price of the attack.

It is best to keep trading options straightforward in most situations. The options trader will calculate the average monthly range of the market to decide whether an option is a good trade or not. It is a figure that gives the promise of uncertainty and the probability of break-even.

They can also compare the average monthly distribution with other similar quantities of stocks. You may see a stock with a good trading opportunity, but the overall range is bad and there is no hope of benefit. Let's presume, however, that you see one that's a little higher than the other, but you know there's a lot of potential for that product. Continuing with the latter is safer because it can mean a potential increase in your own earnings, and it will ultimately benefit you even later as a result.

USING THE AVERAGE MONTHLY RANGE

The trader wants historical prices to measure the average monthly spread. If the stock is picked as the underlying asset, historically high, weak, open and close values can be restored within a certain period of time. The average monthly range includes a certain stock's daily high and low values.

During the time the market fluctuates between the high and low of a given month, the average price can be easily calculated. Conservative traders use the open and close monthly values in most cases. To get the sum, which is then added up and separated by the months, the low price is subtracted from the high price during the month.

[month 1: high price - low price] + [month 2: high price - low price] +

... / (number of months)

A trader should generally consider twice the length of the position in order to arrive at the time frame. Then it's divided into two blocks of time.

Nonetheless, be careful. This approach is not effective when the volatility of the supply assumed makes the premiums irrational. Smaller merchants will be forced to purchase at rates off - the-money strike because they have inadequate resources. To order to be close to the current market price, the average monthly range will advise traders to miss option trading or use a debit spread approach.

At any given time, the average monthly amount can be used on any market. It does not need to be used alone, however. Examination of the business trend must also be used. This idea just makes it impossible for buyers to buy cheap options with far-out - of-the-money that offer limited returns.

BASIC OPTIONS TRADING STRATEGIES

Through options trading, often investors and traders lose money as they exchange options without first knowing their ins and outs. There is a need for a solid strategy to benefit from trade. It allows optimizing a person's income and mitigating risk. To learn how to make use of the strength of choices and their versatility, it takes only a small effort.

THE COVERED CALL

The technique of the Covered Call helps an investor to buy the underlying asset directly. The buyer then has to write and sell a call option on that same asset shortly after the buy. It must be equal to the number of shares.

This approach is used by investors when they have a neutral opinion on the underlying asset for their short-term trading. It is also used by traders who want to protect their investment from any possible value decline. Starting with it is a good basic plan, and if you're worried about losing out on a potential investment, that's the way to go.

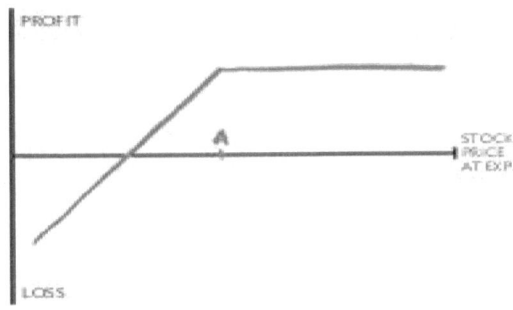

you own the stock (usually at price below A) sell a call strike price A

THE MARRIED PUT

If buyers are bullish about the price of an underlying asset, the Married Put technique is used. We buy the asset's stock initially and then buy a put option of the same number of shares immediately. They do this to protect their investment from potential short-term losses. It's a way to pay on an opportunity at the time, but when it gets tough they don't have to worry about losing something. In a way, there is infinite room for improvements in this.

THE BULL CALL SPREAD

The tactic of Bull Call Spread is used when investors are optimistic about a particular asset and anticipate a modest increase in the price of the underlying asset. At a certain strike price, they purchase a call option, and write and sell a call option at a higher price at the same time. The dealer buys the lower-priced asset when asked, and then sells the higher-priced asset concurrently-thus creating income.

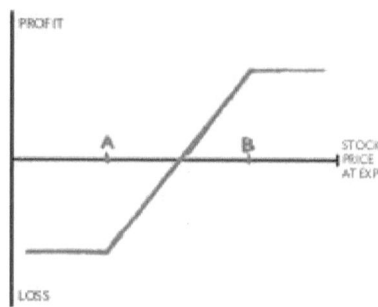

buy a call strike A -- sell a call strike B usually the stock price will be above A and below B

THE BEAR PUT SPREAD

If investors are bearish about the price of an underlying asset, the Bear Put Spread technique is used. They expect the price to fall further in this situation. At a specific price, they purchase a put option, and write and sell another put option at a price below their first option. The trader sells the

higher-priced asset as asked, and re-buys the lower-priced asset at the same time-thus also generating profit.

This will only be effective, like the spread of the bull call, if investors trade the same commodity with a similar expiry date. This technique reduces both profit and loss.

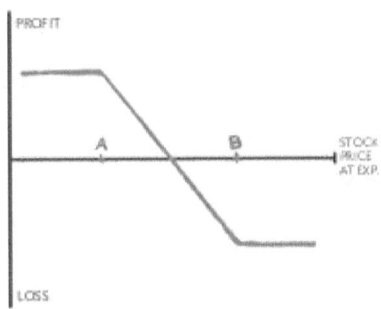

sell a put strike A -- buy a put strike B usually stock price will be at or below B and above A

THE PROTECTIVE COLLAR

The Protective Collar policy locks value without having to sell the underlying asset's stock. Investors buy an option to put out-of-the-money, and write and sell an option to call out-of-the-money. Again, this works only when buyers are concerned with the same asset.

It is used by owners who spend a long time in an underlying asset, gaining income from it. The keep Put option will guarantee gains if the asset price declines. You gain benefit when someone uses the written call option when the asset price increases.

NO DIRECTIONAL OPTIONS TRADING STRATEGIES

1. THE LONG STRADDLE

The technique for the Long Straddle is mainly used to reduce loses and hold profits. In this situation, only the price of the options is limited to the loss. Investors must purchase a position and call option at the same price, the same expiry date, and the same underlying asset to be successful. We use this tactic because we think the asset's price would dramatically change. They're not sure about the path the price will go, though.

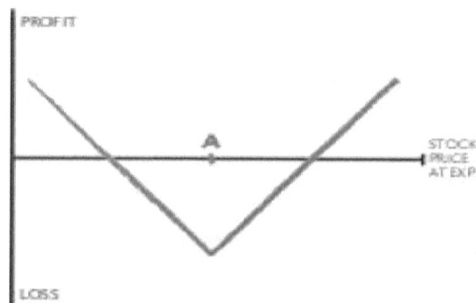

buy a call strike price A -- buy a put strike price A

2. THE LONG STRANGLE

The Long Strangle technique (not to be confused with the previous one) is cheaper than the long straddle because the options are acquired out of the pocket. It is used to reduce losses to the position and call options level. In fact, creditors use this technique because they expect the underlying asset's price will move significantly. They don't know what direction the price is going to move, though.

Investors buy both a position and a call option with the same asset and the same expiry date to be effective, but the options rates vary from each other. The position option's strike price must be below the strike price of the call option. This will result in both the choices being out - of-the-money.

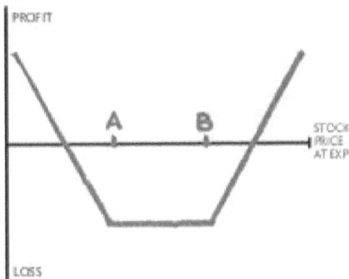

buy a put strike A -- buy a call strike price B usually stock price will be between strike A and strike B

THE BUTTERFLY SPREAD

The technique of the Butterfly Spread is a variation of bear spread and the tactics of the bull spread. This uses different prices as well. A kind of spreading butterfly technique helps buyers to purchase a call option at the lowest price. Instead they write and sell at the same time at a higher price 2 call options and at the highest possible price another call option. So if someone is exercising their right in writing, you're exercising yours promptly. You end up selling high and buying low, contributing to income.

They can also buy a put option at the highest price, then write and sell 2 put options at a lower strike price concurrently, thus selling the last put option at the lowest strike price. So if someone is exercising their right in writing, you're exercising yours promptly. You end up selling high and buying low again- thereby again causing profit.

3. THE IRON CONDOR

The plan for Iron Condor is hard to implement. It's not for buyers with new options as it takes a lot of time and effort to be successful with it. Investors have both a short and long role in two kinds of strangle strategies: a bearish approach and a bullish one.

Yet irrespective of which way, if someone is exercising their written option, you are exercising yours promptly. Completely done, you end up selling high and buying low-inducing income again. Try not to confuse the strike prices when using this alternative technique. You should always wind up with lower orders and higher sales.

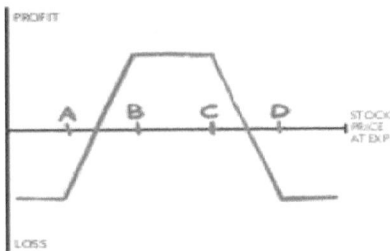

buy a put strike A -- sell a put strike B -- sell a call strike C - buy a call strike D

4. THE IRON BUTTERFLY

A short or long straddle is paired with a strangle by the Iron Butterfly. It's the same as the spread of the butterfly. The distinction, however, is that the iron butterfly simultaneously uses both a put and a call option. Within a certain context, this technique reduces losses and gains. Investors insure that risks are reduced and that the use of out - of-the-money options reduces the risk.

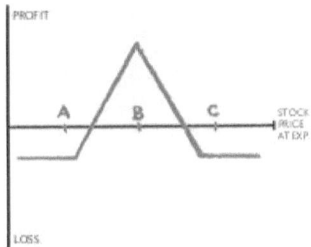

buy a put strike price A - sell a put strike B - sell a call strike B - buy a call strike price C.

CHAPTER 5

AVOIDING MISTAKES IN OPTIONS

TRADING

It is advisable to learn many approaches and boost strong returns over time for new options trader. There are different things to keep in mind when you start options trading. There are errors that can be made, but you will excel in this if you are cautious to avoid the pitfalls.

1. Don't Begin By Purchasing Out-Of-The-Money Call Options.

This technique is often used by other seasoned stock traders who have switched to options trading: purchase a call option and wait to see if it will make a profit. This is similar to the stock trading technique of "buy low, sell high." While it can yield lovely returns in stock trading, this approach does not reliably produce profits in trading options. A seller in options will lose a lot of money in the long run. He may also find that he is not discovering anything new.

An out-of-the-money option is a cheap investment because the premium depends on the probability of it hitting or moving beyond the strike price. This chance is small in most cases. So the option's price is also small.

Instead of drafting and selling an out-of-the-money call option on the underlying asset currently owned by a new options broker. When the call option is exercised, the asset must be sold by the contract owner. The writer will make a profit from the right because of this duty. If the buyer is bullish about the asset, he/she will be able to earn more money-ready to sell the stock even as the price increases before the option expires. Do not invest directly, but instead sell and write call options to make a profit as a result.

2. Watch The Timing

It seems impossible to predict how a stock's price would rise in stock trading. The same relates to options trading. The fluctuation will occur overnight several times before you even think about it. The alternative can spike in price, so you need to watch for any market changes.

Typically a trader has to forecast the course of price movement accurately. At first they may not be accurate, but being able to see the difference will save you so many headaches, and as a result you will know about where the options are going to trade. He/she must also forecast the right time, however, that the price will move in the direction predicted.

If a trader with a right to call makes an error on either or both dimensions, he/she will forfeit the premium paid. If the underlying asset takes a long time to move in the direction predicted, as the expiry date approaches, the income gets lower. Therefore, you should know where it will happen, and the approximate timing of the existence of a stock's direction. See where it's going to fall, and as a result, you will decide where you'll end up.

3. Try Covered Calls

There is really nothing dangerous about using the covered call technique to trade calls. The risk remains in the ownership of the underlying asset; a buyer may lose an amount equal to the disparity between the underlying asset's prevailing market price and the premium option.

The loss may be significant in most cases. When drafting and selling the contract, there is no capital cost. There is chance of investment, though, because there is a small payoff to the buyer. The buyer will use the right when the price of the underlying asset soars. The retailer is losing potential gain as such. On the other hand, since the purchaser holds the underlying asset, the asset price must have risen to the strike price of the contract.

The writer/seller retains the long position on a flat market when earning the premium alternative. If the writer wants to go out after the asset's price has dropped, he / she will actually buy the right back to close the short position. In fact, to close the long position, the writer should sell the underlying asset. By closing the role, he / she can suffer losses. The covered call selling is a low-risk and wise tactic for traders of new options. It can be used by a seller in options as he/she becomes more familiar with trading options.

4. Don't Use An "All-Purpose" Strategy For Every Market Condition

Dealing options versatility allows traders and investors to engage in dealing under all market conditions. When they try to learn other techniques, they can do so. In different market conditions, they can buy spreads.

There is actually a right requirement on the market to use it, however. There are two options for a long spread position: selling the lower-cost option and purchasing a higher-cost alternative. Only the strike price varies from these shares. A long spread of the call is a positive posture (thinking the price of the asset will rise) when bearish a long spread (thinking the price of the asset will fall). The time downside of one alternative may be a time advantage of the other when selling a spread. The problem of spacing is therefore compensated by spreads.

However, the disadvantage of spreads is that the investor's upside potential is limited. In reality, not many people earn enormous profits from spreads. But there's also limited potential damage. Strategies that may be "all-purpose" may seem like a good idea, but sometimes doing it can obscure an investment's true potential. You may make more of one type of investment than another. At first, many don't know that, but that's because they end up seeing an opening they lost. Try calls for ideal circumstances and learn what to do in any situation.

5. If "Middle Men" Are Involved

When spreading dealings investors and traders must be vigilant. For brokers, spread trading can pay a lot of commissions because different trades are involved in this type of trading. They must include fees in the balance in the profit/loss estimate. Ultimately, they need to know the risks of the commissioner deals, which will include a share of the profits. Sometimes a commissioner's net loss can be up to 30%, which is a lot if you look at how much you put in as a premium. Don't depend on intermediaries to make a profit. You can find online cheap broker sites, but also make sure they are a legitimate place to use, as there are often fake broker sites, which could result in an even greater loss of money.

6. Have An Exit Plan Before The Option Expires

There is no place for feelings in options trading. Traders and investors need a strategy to be effective in it, and they need to stick to executing it. There are upside and down exits to a good exit plan; there are also time frames for each escape. Having a plan produces effective habits of trade which causes people not to think.

A dealer in new options will know the amount of income that will please himself enough. The dealer always needs to know how much risk he or she is willing to take. The dealer always needs to know all quantities ahead of time. When the profit is reached, it is necessary to clear the position. The same goes for the target of the downside.

7. Don't "Double Up" To Recover Past Losses

Options traders often consider themselves in defiance of their own laws in most situations. It may be possible to double in stock trading in order to recover the losses. If the price is low, a stock investor can buy more shares. This may not, however, be true of trading options.

There are different options than stocks. Therefore, in trading options, "double up" doesn't make sense. Time loss must always be taken into account. When trading options, leverage is important. It can also lead the trader to lose significantly, however. Reducing damages and closing the place is important to avoid a catastrophe.

8. Be Careful With Trading Illiquid Options

A liquid market is perfect for option traders as it is easy to transact at all times when there are both sellers and buyers. It also guarantees the sale of the next exchange at a price that is the same as the last one.

Generally speaking, the stock market has more liquidity than the options market, as the latter offers more opportunities than the former. An investors opting to buy illiquid options will pay a higher premium than the options ' usual cost.

Generally speaking, it is prudent to sell open-interest options at least 40 times the number of option contracts you want to trade. For starters, if an investor wants to trade 10 lots, at least 400 contracts should be his or her liquidity. Transacting liquid alternatives is the best way.

9. Don't Waste A Lot Of Time To Decide To Buy Back Short Options

A seller in options must always be willing to buy back short options. Most of the time, as he/she may not like to pay commissions, the trader cannot decide early. The seller may assume that without the investor exercising it, the contract would automatically terminate.

Finally, the dealer may be expecting to benefit from the contract even a little bit. Buying back the short alternative is better than suffering the chance of being out of the capital. In fact, if there is still at least 80 percent of the benefit from the initial option offer, the buyer will buy back the short option. Difficulty to do this will result in damages.

10. Dividend Payment Dates And Earnings Must Be Included In The Options Strategy

An options trader will track the underlying asset's payout dates and earnings. Owners with shares are unable to take advantage of distributions. If a big payout is declared, they will use a call option to purchase the underlying asset-thereby collecting the dividends.

While early assignment is hard to control because it's pretty random, it's better for options traders to detect any imminent dividends and prevent early assignment. For fact, the season of earnings increases the price of contract options. Any news of the underlying asset could improve volatility. Trading options are recommended after results release has already passed.

Dividends awaiting increase the risk of redistribution. Any investor, even with a pending dividend, who still wants to trade options, will know about the ex-dividend date. For fact, the season of earnings raises option rates and uncertainty. Any trader who still wants to trade options this season may want to build a spread by holding on an option for a long time and going short on another. During the earnings season, the price of the underlying asset is usually inflated. As such, buyers should expect prime options to be distorted as well.

11. If Assigned Early, The Options Trader Must Know What To Do

An options trader of who writes short options must know that assignment can be made. Traders of new options often do not consider assignment. So the effect can be devastating when it happens to them. When their short options are issued, many new options traders can panic. It is best to remain realistic in most situations and think about the best ways to get out of the situation.

Traders need to find it early in order to cope with an early assignment. If not, they would often find themselves making decisions that are irrational and defensive. It is possible to consider business research. Traders should weigh the advantages and disadvantages of calling or calling early. They may get cash if they exercise a put or sell a stock. Traders are now going to prefer cash to wait for expiration at times. It ensures that often a position decision is exercised early than an option to call. However, if the underlying asset is expected to pay dividends, this may not be the case.

If a call is executed, the underlying asset can now be bought by traders then waiting for expiration. They'd rather wait in most cases. Inexperienced traders may exercise this option early if the underlying asset's price has risen. They did not realize that if they exercise early, they were wasting time premium.

12. In Trading A Spread, Don't "Leg In"

Most option traders, including experienced ones, are learning the hard way. They take an additional market risk that is needless. What they should do is work with a spread as if it were a special transaction. All markets have to be developed concurrently. A spread can't be run without first gaining net credit or debit. This is the perfect way to mitigate risks and bring the technique into practice. Take one spread to watch the market at a time. An excessive risk will ruin your opportunity to invest in the future, and if you are not vigilant with the dangers and drawbacks of a plan, it could cause significant damage.

13. For Neutral Trades, Use Index Options

There is uncertainty in every stock. If a big surprise press release is issued by the publicly listed company, the stock price will certainly be impacted for a few days. A single company, though, may not be able to greatly influence the index.

Trading shares using indexes is a good way to protect traders in a particular company from any major movement. It is recommended that if traders do not want to care about the effect of a single news on the price of an underlying asset, they do balanced trades dependent on global indices.

Long indices spreads can be lucrative if the demand stagnates. Any unexpected news about a particular company will affect the price of its stock drastically and rapidly. In most cases, the stock is going to sell as an after-effect in a new horizon. On the other hand, there are different movements of indices. It's less emotional. More often than not, a single change in an organization does not affect them.

14. Master The Spread

A short spread of separate strike prices can include 2 positions. The higher price alternative is offered while the lower price option is acquired. Except for the size, the two alternatives must have the same parameters. They have to be both calls or both puts. In fact, they must have the same contract length, expiry date, and underlying assets. It is possible to mitigate the ill effects of timing because one is sold and the other is bought.

A significant difference between short and long spreads is that when there is a common underlying asset, the former is designed to be competitive. A short put spread can therefore be favorable to positive while the short calls can be neutral to bear. In fact, there must be at least one trading option for the spreads. This means dealers are going to have to pay more than one fee for brokers.

Understanding and learning each of the spreads will assist you in making good investment decisions. You will know when to call or scatter, and you will be able to determine whether or not something is worth investing in. Many occasions when one starts, because of the imminent opportunity and the changes they see, they can call on something. If they do that, though, and the market crashes, they will eventually lose what they have invested. It's best to put the premium risk as your main risk, and if you feel comfortable when you keep learning the spreads, you're going to be successful.

15. Continue Learning

Options trading can be very difficult for most people and intimidating. Capital can be lost in it, particularly if the trader is the seller because if the buyer wants to exercise the option, he/she has an obligation to fulfill it. On the other hand, before the contract expires, the buyer has a right, not an obligation, to use the option. This can be a frightening endeavor for most people, especially the inexperienced.

We fail to realize, though, that they can know anything. Just before they try to trade on their own, they have to waste time and effort studying options trading. A wealth of information on options trading is open. All that's required is to find the information, read, then exchange for an interested investor.

Options trading can be dangerous. But by making the right decisions, it is possible to mitigate the harm. A person needs to know how to trade options before he/she can make a reasonable decision.

CHAPTER 6

INTERMEDIATE RISK MEASUREMENT: DELTA, GAMMA, THETA, VEGA, RHO, LAMBDA

The Different Types of Immediate Risk Management

Now that you know about the different models and how you're going to use options trading, it's time to talk about the patterns that may emerge from trading options. There are different ways of how the economy works with the changes in the market. This is important to learn because when learning about market fluctuations, certain words are often used. This chapter will discuss what each of the five major definitions is, along with a few examples of what they are doing in the market when it happens in certain circumstances.

DELTA

Delta is the word for change in Greece. In options trading, it means changing the underlying asset's price to the associated interest derivative shift. It is sometimes referred to as the "hedge ratio." Let's say, for instance, that an asset's price is going to be.8. This means $1 of the underlying stock raise indefinitely, and $.80 would increase the call option. The delta usually increases the more the stock hits the option's expiration. It will reach a delta of 1.00 at the end of it.

An example of this when using trading options is if you buy an out-of- money call or position option, the option will have a 1.0—1.0 delta interest. At-the-money ones sometimes go from.5 to-.5. It is not a constant, but it is associated with other measurements of risk, and it will show the rate of delta change given by the underlying. Delta is also subject to the volatility implied, so it is not entirely reliable.

With this, when you take your portfolio of options into account, you can calculate the net-long or net-short of something along with the underlying.

GAMMA

Gamma presents you with an approximation of how the variance adjusts when the price moves $1. This can tell you how the delta is "stable." It means that if there is a major gamma, the delta will begin to change drastically for every slight step. You get a good gamma if there's a long call or a long place. Quick puts and calls on the other side of the coin transform the gradient into a negative one. Always change storage so it's got 0 gamma.

The gamma graph changes just as the delta does. It usually looks like a slope, with the top close to the blast. For ATM choices, Gamma is the largest. It means that when stock prices rise, the ATM options will adjust the most. You can see the variability as you see how the gamma shifts based on the type of option. The passage of time on a gamma graph will serve as a "pulling up" to the end. Nevertheless, as the option expires, the gamma tends to decline along with the uncertainty.

What that means is a good position with a positive gamma. If it goes up, it will produce the deltas that help move the stock, but if it is bad, it can damage you regardless of whether it goes up or down. Gamma lets you look at your position's profit / loss ratio over a wide variety of stock prices. Negative gamma positions can be dangerous, so not playing with them is critical.

THETA

Theta indicates the reduction over time; it is an indicator of how much an option declines as one day passes and when the supply or price is not rising. Theta indicates how much the value of the right decreases as time goes by. It's always changing, but it shows how quickly everything changes. Nevertheless, the theta is not equivalent for the call and set at the same strike price. The difference between calling and placing theta depends on the stock's rate. If the stock's output is low, the call theta is greater than the put. The theta is smaller than the put if the stock is negative.

There's always a negative theta for long calls and fast puts. There's a good theta for short calls and puts. Nevertheless, stock has zero theta, indicating that with time it is not diminished. Theta measures the gap in an option's extrinsic worth with more expiry days to one with fewer expiry days. Long options have a negative theta and there is a positive theta for short options. If the option loses value on an ongoing basis, however, a short option will create a positive theta to make money, but a long one will have the ability to lose money.

When time goes by, the theta's rate is rising. It begins to increase in theta when it is closer to the end of the option, but if it is further away, it decreases more slowly. That's why you need to take advantage of the interest of an opportunity early on, because if you don't, you won't get all the money for it.

Because of the high extrinsic interest, Theta is the highest for ATM options, and the theta of higher and variable options is lower before expiration. Gamma and theta are opposites, and it will have a high negative theta if something has a high positive gamma. In a way, gamma is something that has the power to make money if the product starts to move significantly. Theta, however, is what you're paying for all that strength, and the longer the stock doesn't move, the more it hurts your spot.

VEGA

Vega is not represented by a letter from Greece, but it is still very relevant. It is an estimate of how much of an option's theoretical value if volatility changes by 1%. The higher the volatility, the higher the price of the option. A higher volatility is tossing the stock price, generating a probability that the sale will make money.

Long calls and puts have a good Vega as time goes on because it shifts. Stock has no Vega because the uncertainty does not affect it. A positive Vega means that the position of the option increases as stability increases and decreases as uncertainty increases. Often, Vega can rise as uncertainty increases, and ITM and OTM are higher options. This means it will have a higher Vega if you have a choice that is changing a lot.

RHO

Rho is an indicator of how much an option's value changes as interest rates rise 1%. The rho for a call and the same strike price and the same month of expiration are not the same. It is the Greeks ' least-used message, and it is one of the methods of choices that is not used as much as the other. If an economy's interest rates are high, the probability of an option position will fall due to how weak it is.

Long calls and short puts have a positive rho, but short calls and long puts have a negative rho. The reason this happens is that the valuation of an option is dependent on the cost of holding a stock position. It has to do with the fact that an option is a stock inventory swap. If the stock trades for a higher interest, you'll have a higher rho, and if holding a stock position is more lucrative, the more expensive the call option will be. But if interest rates go down, the value of calls will go up and the value of puts will go down. A fall in interest rates decreases calls value and raises put value.

LAMBDA

Lambda is the amount of percentage change in the price of an option contract relative to the percentage change in the actual price of that same option. Lambda is one of the Greeks used in the study of derivatives. For a percentage point change in its implied volatility, Lambda measures the change in an option premium. The option's price will be more prone to the small changes in value when the lambda is high. If the lambda is small, the variance shifts will have less impact on the value of the contract.

Lambda is the delta by-product because the ratio of the base demand to the contract price changes. Because the relationship with delta is clear and not moving, it is not commonly used. Traders tend to use delta as it explicitly provides them with their risk profile. Lambda deals with the selling of products to consumers. A lambda's value is about 5-15. It is prone to maturity preference, although for money options it is quite significant.

LET'S PUT THIS INTO PRACTICAL

In the field of options trading in the form of illustrations, the best way to understand something of this type is to see how it is done. There are some examples above, but this section will show only a few aspects that selling options can be used and how it will impact the use of various options and what happens when you position calls and orders.

For delta, let's take stock X as an example. Let's say the value of X is $3 and the value of the delta is.4. With the stock price at $48. Now let's say stock is rising to $49, a pound. The interest would grow to $3.40 if that happens. And if it drop, $2.60 will be the value. It can be used in the same manner as other figures, such as if the stock is priced at $4.00 and the differential is valued at $48 with the stock at-.5. Let's presume the stock is rising, it's going to fall to $3.50 instead of growing the decision. But if for some reason it increases, it's going to go up to $4.50. It's an interesting way it falls, and even if the stock price doesn't change, the changes can happen.

For Gamma, an example is if you've got stock X with a.40 delta for the order, but the put has-.5 with a $48 mark. For both of these, the gamma is

0.07. Then, if it moves, it's going to become the gamma, plus the price rise, and then the deltas. with a call and a put, it goes the same way, so you can see how the stock moves as a result. the position of the delta moves as the stock prices jump by a dollar is determined for the gamma position.

For theta, how a stock can decline over time is an example. Let's assume, for instance, we have a stock priced at $4.00. Let's offer this stock at the expiry of 20 days and a-.15 theta. It's worth $4.75 to bring on this portfolio and it has 80 days until it expires at-.05 with a theta. Now let's assume the day passes and the stock price does not change, and the option's uncertainty does not indicate any change. The put will drop to $3.85 at the end of that day, while the other will only be $4.70. It means that at first the stock that has less time to mature will lose less revenue, but then as time goes on it will grow larger.

The theta location will calculate the shift value as a day goes by. It is measured just like the delta, but only using the one-point value for the contract option. Typically these are about $100, but because of the way the stock breaks, they can be different. The option of theta is measured in the position, compounded by the number of contracts and the value of one point for the contract option, and then added together. For Vega, in a call you can see an indication of this. It could be worth $2.00 and a Vega of +.20 with price turnover of 30%. If the variance goes up to 31 percent, the interest will go up to $2.20. Now let's assume that for some reason the Vega fell down to 29 cents, then the stock's value drops to $1.80. The Vega is assessed by 1 percent change. A theta location is determined in the same way. The Vega is determined, weighted for each option contract by the number of contracts and the dollar value at one point. It is then put together.

For rho, you can see this in your handling of the warehouse. Let's say you think a stock will rise, so for $4800 you get 100 shares, or you can get 2 calls for $400. Now, let's assume there's a+.8 delta position above a 100 delta position. You'd have to pay about twelve times the price you'd invest on stock options, which means you'd have to borrow money on interest to even get the stock, and that's typically measured in the valuation of an offer.

So, let's assume there's a stock that has 50 calls at @2.00 and a.2 rho with a stock at $48 and a 5 percent interest. Now if it increases by 1%, the amount will only increase to $2.02, and if it drops, it will go down to $1.98.

All of these terms support you in the selling of shares. In the next segment, we will explore the different ways of using each of these different strategies of choices and how they influence how risk management is generated. We are important to know, and all options traders need to hear about it.

BASIC TECHNIQUES FOR RISK MANAGEMENT

Risk management for options traders is very relevant. It's something any investor options will know about, and if you don't, it can later create problems. This section will discuss some of the best risk management strategies for active traders to help avoid any snags later when it comes to options trading. In addition, once you understand them, you can use them to protect your money, and now and later that will save you a lot of problems.

WHY PREPARE ?

You may ask why this is something you need to know. First of all, it is an important part of trading options that many people overlook. There are lots of derivatives traders coming into it, doing some sales, and ending up getting big gains from it. That's great, but if you don't use the proper risk management over time and don't use it, you can lose it all in two bad trades. Such easy tactics maximize the earnings and are something any trader should learn about

PLANNING TRADES

The first thing you have to do is prep with everything in life. Through battles to what you're going to do later, how you come out on top is planning and preparation. It is the preparation that will get you somewhere, and effective traders are preparing their business before any sort of trading starts. The distinction between defeat and disappointment is to plan ahead.

Stop-loss and take-profit are two ways to help selling options plan ahead. A seller knows the price they are willing to pay to sell options, and they calculate the return against the possibility that the supply will meet the number predicted. They're going to trade it if they get enough out of it.

Successful traders don't even glance at what they're dealing on, or have a schedule when to sell to get a return. They don't know how the trading prices will change, and as a result, with the options they have, they're like gamblers. You may have an unfair streak and then control over feelings. Emotions are not part of trading shares, they are just planning and policy. If errors arise, people hold on to and decide that they want their money back, but then they keep making the same mistakes. You're going to end up coming out on top of the deal if you intend before you sell.

STOP-LOSS AND TAKE-PROFIT EXPLAINED

You have seen above what these two words are, but you ought to know what they mean. It's crucial to have a firm grasp of this, because as a broker, it can be the determining factor of making the deal and income, and you can't.

A stop-loss is the price the trader is going to sell a stock and lose the trading. It happens when the trade is not as they were expecting. These will help prevent the mindset of "it's going to come back" and reduce the loses before it gets work. For e.g., if the stock breaks before a point, it will be sold by a dealer as quickly as possible to avoid losing anything.

A take profit is the same price that a trader sells stock to make a profit. It's when they want the opportunity to hit the mark. It's when, given the risks, the upside is limited. If the stock goes up to a level of resistance, it will be sold by an options broker before the meeting takes place.

HOW TO SET UP STOP-LOSS POINTS

You will try to set up opportunities to avoid loses and make profits. Typically this is achieved by calculations with a technical analysis, but you should also look at the basic analysis as well. For instance, if a trader keeps a stock ahead of earnings as he generates anticipation, he might want to sell it off before the market knows about it. This will discourage more from investing in it, and before it becomes too expensive they will make a return from it.

Changing percentages are another way to do this. This is easy to calculate and is market-driven to track. Typically they are achieved by some timed averages. You should place this on the map of a stock to assess when the price has changed and when it is at a level of support or resistance.

You can also calculate this, and configure trendlines to be set up. They can be made by connecting a significant volume to the highs and lows that occurred. Such rates are reacting to the trendlines and generating a high volume. Nonetheless, you can ensure that you use this with volatile stocks in the long term to avoid price fluctuations that trigger a stop-loss. You should change the averages to the product points you want and reduce the number of signals by the longer thresholds. You should also respond to the fluctuations of the market. If the price is not going, then it is possible to extend the stop-loss point. To order to increase stock price, you should also look at key time intervals.

CALCULATING RETURNS

Another way to help you measure the expected return is to set up pause and take points. It's important, because instead of rationalizing it, you can think with the cost. It will also give you asystematic way at the most competitive time to compare trades and sell. This will give you a chance to see what will be the expected return. It will help to determine when to sell, along with the probability of gain or loss, and help make educated guesses.

Such techniques for risk management will help prevent things from getting worse. Understanding this is important, and it's something any investor can take in before they start trading in options. It lowers the risk and lets you get out on top.

RISKS IN OPTIONS TRADING

There are some risk management tools used with trading options that can help you plan better and make things better for you. This section will go through nine different things to watch out for when trading options, and why trading options are relevant for each of these nine choices. To maintain stability in options trading, you should be able to use this along with considerable success.

ALLOCATION FLOWS DOWNSTREAM

The first definition is the division of asset. You will make sure you don't bring it all together. You should ensure that you do not invest your entire portfolio in equities, but also in bonds, real estate, and commodities. They should also work to ensure that communities are also protected by the diversification.

Many start thinking they're only going to put their options on stocks like Apple or Google. If you don't bring it elsewhere, though, it will make your investments in one region too weighted. Additionally, you can make sure it doesn't conflict with each other as if you own both stocks and mutual funds. Before investing in it, you should look at the company and what they hold, as you may end up investing too much in one area.

The reason you should watch for this and make sure you allocate effectively is because when volatility occurs, the more diverse a portfolio means fewer swings or losses will occur. However, the downturns can be correlated in recent years, so make sure you don't put everything in one market if you're investing. When you put everything in real estate, it may end up ruining you, like the case of a lot of investors collapsing during the 2008 housing bubble.

1. THE IMPORTANCE OF DIFFERENCES

Diversified options will actually make a difference in a portfolio. Options can be seen as a class, particularly those that are volatile. You can also be used in general to shield you. They can use ETFs to support me, and when it comes to hedging, it can be useful. Having a different portfolio can help prevent something wrong from happening, and it can also illustrate that if things go wrong, you are in a good position.

2. WATCHING OVERALL RISK CAPITAL

You have to look out for the risk capital as a whole. If you are options for trading, you will wait for it to grow above 15-20 percent of the total risk capital. That's because if you let it go beyond that, you put yourself at risk and you may have too much on the table. You will also need to prepare in case you may risk more of your money than planned if the stop-loss happens to you. That's why you should make sure your fund has only that much, and act accordingly if it meets that.

3. WATCH OPTION ACCOUNT

If you have an option account, you need to look at how much is available on the market. You should ensure that at any time there is no more than 50 percent on the market. Even having 50 percent on the market is risky, so if you can, it might be best to have less than that.

4. WATCH SINGULARITIES

You will make sure, for a single option, that it does not constitute more than 5 percent of the risk side options portfolio. If that position begins to fail, if it is that number, it won't hurt you. That's because it will typically fall down to only 2.5%, which is just a reduction of 50%. Making sure you don't put too much in one place is better than relying on one choice to save everything.

5. TRADE HOW YOU'RE COMFORTABLE

The issue with many beginner traders is that they are not dealing with what they are familiar with. Most credit products are difficult to understand, but the main issue at hand is that they are goods with double collateral. Many who are beginning with their building and actions are not confident. You should make sure you know how to deal with the drug, because if you don't care enough about it, you won't get anywhere with it. It can save you if you carry this risk management technique in, and it can make the ability to trade options even easier by mixing this with understanding.

6. MANAGE YOUR MONEY

Managing money for this is critical. You just have to use a certain number, so you need to keep control of it to prevent it being lost forever. Position-size is the best thing to do, when you decide how much you want to invest in any shares. By doing so, you will decide how much you are going to invest and how much of an amount you are going to put into something. You can use only a small amount so that you don't depend on one result. Many enterprises can turn out to be bad, but if you handle it properly and only invest a certain amount into it, you will be able to decide how much you will bring in and how bad the possible risks can be.

7. MANAGE ORDERS

If you want to manage the risk in a simple but effective way, you can choose to put different options. Along with the four key order types, you can place orders to assist with risk management in various options. They can look at what's going to help they, and this can also help prevent you from selling at a lower price. To order to reduce profits, there are instructions you can instantly lock in a return. For example, if you use a limit stop button, these can monitor when you leave the role. This will help to avoid the situations where you lose out on income from keeping too long a position, or it will eliminate any major losses because you have not blackout quickly enough.

8. WATCHING OPTIONS SPREADS

Checking the options spread of will give you a clear idea of how the market moves. For instance, if you purchased some calls on a stock and then wrote on the same stock cheaper money calls, it ends up being a spread of bull calling. Such spreads should be used to help manage risks. In addition to reducing how much you want to use, you can reduce the costs of joining a position, ad this can help to minimize the overall risk.

Such spreads will also help with short positions, and they are all outlined to you, as explained earlier. It can be used to decide when to exit, and even how the business trend is going. This can avoid defeats, and in the long run it can save you. For anyone trying to reduce the costs of multiple options trading, these spreads are important, and they are very important to know.

Trading options might seem like a huge, complicated business, but minimizing the trading options risks is how you put yourself in a position where you know what's going to come out of it and what's going to happen. Doing so will help minimize costs and help optimize the profits you want in selling the options.

CHAPTER 7

OPTIONS TRADING SECRETS AND RECOVERING FROM LOSSES

It will sound like you're bombarded with a lot of details when you start trading for options. This is real. But if you want to get the momentum right from the start to stop those defeats for beginners, you need to have a few tricks up your sleeve to gain an advantage. Because at the end of the day, the only thing that will bring you the money you want is the benefits/leverages.

While most people may think there are some sort of "secrets" that make rich people wealthy and don't let the other trading compete. But it can't be far from the facts. In fact, all the secrets you're going to read here are common sense, and all rely on your ability to recognize and apply certain things.

Patience and self-discipline are the biggest secret to everything (yes, including life). You want to make sure that with every exchange you learn new things and that the understanding of a particular topic is constantly growing. You will be tested in this way, but in a challenging and positive manner.

1. Never Think In Dollar Amounts. Think In Terms Of Fixed Percentages

This is one of the big mistakes even moderate traders make—they tend to think about the dollar amounts they're going to profit or lose on any deal.

When you think about trading in dollar amounts, you're going to think you're going to make at least $2 for every $1 you've got in your trading account. And let's say you've got a $5,000 budget. Common sense says you already have $2 on the table, which can go both directions—either turning it into a profit or making it into a loss. And that also includes the $1 original.

Then you decide to put $500 on the table for every $1 and make a profit of $2. Simple calculation suggests that running out of money will only take 10 bad trades. On the other hand, you'll be stopping yourself from taking a lot of chance if you conceive of these things in terms of a fixed percentage. Yeah, you'll only lose $150 a deal if you want to invest 3 percent of your overall capital to make a profit. Of course that also means that as your portfolio increases, the amount you will lose will increase.

And, by thinking in terms of a fixed percentage, and not in dollar amounts, save yourself from taking huge risks.

2. Hedge, Hedge, Hedge

Hedging is one of the most important trading aspects of options. Imagine, for starters, taking an opposing position and keeping the current position as well. When you think the stock will go higher after that investment, you can simply buy 10 call options for profit. But what if a game is played against you by the cosmos and the stock is not going higher? As the options expire, you will end up losing the money.

But with hedging, should things go against you, you can turn the loss into a benefit by buying 5 put options. And, even if things are going extremely poorly for you, with a bonus in hand you can still come out of it.

One hedging technique is called a covered call. You own the underlying stock in this strategy, so you make a bid on that stock. By selling the offer, you decide to cover the option of selling the stock at the strike price. It means that when things hit the fan, the loss on your investments is transformed into the commodity, resulting in you spending less money.

With every trade, one thing you should know is that you should use everything in your arsenal and have as much leverage as you can to make a profit. Using various techniques and choices that you have. Besides, take advantage of the insurance you get from trading options.

3. There Is Never An "All-Purpose" Strategy

Traders and investors who pursue a single strategy irrespective of the market conditions are typically those who are intimidated by the stock market. They continue to invest and don't sell unless the conditions change tremendously. If you want to make a quick profit and avoid long-term risks, that's totally wrong.

Even, as some traders say, there is never an "all-purpose" approach. You need to go with the tide and adjust to market conditions in this situation. In fact, let market conditions lead you in the right direction. You're going to come out with a boost more often than not.

It means you should never miss any calls, spreads and places buying opportunities. But of course, before you buy any of that, you should know what's going on in the economy. The work comes into play here.

4. Always Have An Exit Strategy

You should always be in front of the curve and have in place an exit strategy. Whether you win or lose doesn't matter. If things go south, a good exit strategy will help you to limit your losses. Moreover, it also helps you unstuck some of the trades that keep sucking in your money. The exit strategy, on the other hand, always protects you from losing profits in the future. For any type of investment, this law is fundamental. You want to make sure that with a smile and a decent amount you can get out of the case.

5. Research Before Doubling Down

Doubling your profits is tempting when you know a trade is going according to your plan. But then there are always bad things going on. And that's why you'd like to make sure you're ahead of the game.

You're working out the patterns and then trying to avoid losses. Make sure you know there's a strong pattern and you can trust it to make your income. Even after that, if things go south, you should have an exit plan to save yourself. Always play attract when it comes to trading options because you're going to end up losing your portfolio.

Opening a new trading account options may be quick, but it's not worth the effort. Before you launch, you will try to stay low and learn to rope and slowly increase the risks you take. And you'll be able to live a corporate lifestyle over time.

6. Never Start Trading With Out-Of-The-Money (Otm) Call Options

It may seem like the right thing to do on the surface, but it's more of a bet and less of a company. Buying small and selling high feels right because that's the business / trading mindset we all have. But you see, trading options are much more relevant than just buying low and selling high. There are a lot of other leverages that you may need to reliably increase those earnings. OTM calls are one of the greatest errors made by newbies doing options trading. They don't know that making money on a consistent level is one of the toughest forms.

So what's wrong with buying calls?

Calling the path in which the stock should travel takes a lot of work and stamina. Not only do you need to be right about the route, but you also need to be right about that direction's pacing. You forfeit the fee you pay for that right if anything goes against that.

And when things go south, the stock doesn't shift in your desired direction every day, just sitting under the sun evaporates your opportunity. It'll wait for the expiration date every day because you can't do much.

Selling an OTM call on a stock that you already own is what you can do to have an educated exchange in this case. In terms of trading futures, this is considered "covered call." What you essentially agree on is that if the strike price is higher than the current stock price, and if the stock price hits or goes beyond the strike price within the specified duration, you will have no duty to sell the stock to the buyer if they order it.

You're going to make some money by selling your OTM call when you do this. And if the price of the stock exceeds the price of the shot, you will earn even more income.

The selling of your OTM call reduces the risk and places the stock itself at risk. It means you won't gamble as much as you would if you hadn't sold the OTM call even though the chance is significant.

But if the stock price does not hit the strike price and the economy is stable, you're not going to lose anything and you're going to collect the offer to deliver the bid as well. Finally, before you sell the OTM order, you'll have your long stock spot.

On the other hand, by selling covered calls, if you become acquainted with the field of options trading, you can learn the ropes even faster and without losing a lot of money. Selling covered calls is considered a good tactic because the cost is very small, while you can still make significant money.

In fact, you'll also learn how option prices respond to small stock fluctuations and how prices decrease over time.

7. Trading Illiquid Options

Liquidity is critical if you want to make quick money. Liquidity means a market is open and at all stages there are already willing buyers and sellers. The statistical definition of liquidity will be: the chance of performing the next transaction at a price equal to the last.

By fact, stock markets are more competitive than trading options. This is because only one type of stock is traded by stock traders. While options traders, on the other hand, have plenty of contracts from which they can choose.

For example, only one type of IBM stock will have to be purchased by a stock trader that is it. On the other hand, an options dealer will have a lot of expiry dates to choose from and a bucket load of strike prices. This means the market trading stocks are not as competitive as the stock market. But IBM does not have to do anything with the liquidity in options trading or the stock market.

Let's take another example of a smaller company than IBM. Together with IBM, Superior-Processors portfolios will be much more dormant, and the options will be even more inactive. Superior-Processors is a fictional processing processor business that claims that in 5 years ' time the world will use quantum processors in their daily lives. But as they are a small business, their stocks are sold only once a week and only by invitation.

When the stocks become idle, the options ' offer and request price is excessively high. For eg, if the bid-ask spread is $0.30

(bid=$1.90, ask=$2.20), and if you're buying the $2.20 deal, you're setting up a losing situation right off the bat. However, because of the lack of liquidity in the market for that particular stock, you will also have a lot of issues to deal with.

Once you start trading in options, the best thing you can do for yourself is to swap liquid options. This will not only help you save a lot of time, energy and stress, but in a short amount of time it will also help you learn a lot more.

8. Never Wait Too Long To Buy Back Your Short Options

It doesn't matter if you're just hoping you'd be able to squeeze out that tiny trade profit, or you're just waiting for a worthless contract to expire. To buy back your short options, you should never wait too long. It's much better to buy short options early than to focus on why you made the same mistake again.

If you think a deal gets out of hand and you can buy back the short option to cut the risk and finish the transaction with a boost, then do that right away. The extra money you pay will be worth it.

For example, if you had an option of $1.00 and its value dropped to 20 cents today, you wouldn't sell it because it's not worth it. You shouldn't also worry about scratching out a few cents to benefit from that deal.

The best thing you can do is to buy back the short option immediately to save your 80 percent from leaving. Because it's only a matter of time when the quick option comes around like karma and you bite just because you've been waiting too long to buy it back.

9. Never Fail To Include The Earnings Or Dividend Payments Dates In Your Options Strategy

You want to know when the payout approaches the underlying stock, because as the holders of the shares, you have no right to a stock dividend. To obtain the dividend, bond rights must be exercised and the underlying shares must be bought.

Keeping track of these dates should work for you and avoid the risk of early transfer. You'll see that being allocated is a random thing that happens in the next hidden and it's a threat to traders in options. Imminent dividends are one of the few variables that can be detected and minimized to reduce your chances of being distributed.

When you imagine this in the circumstances of the real world, you will know that contract options will become pricier during the season of earnings. Agreement solutions are like benefits. If you want to get home insurance in Florida and the weather forecast says you're headed for a storm, then it's clear your insurance is going to be very expensive compared to other cases. The same happens for contract options. They get costly during the season of earnings.

If you like high volatility securities trading, the earnings season is going to be the best time to do that. But you should also have a mentality that there will be many ups and downs, and you will have to gain a lot of power to remain above the surface. To be on a safe side as an investor, after the release of results and the consequences have been absorbed by the market, you want to swap options. If you want to witness uncertainty and know, by purchasing just one option and selling the other, you can stay safe. This is going to create a break.

How is that going to help you? Because of the earning season, the price of the option you're going to buy is probably inflated. But due to the season, the price of the option you're going to sell will also be high.

10. Know What To Do When You're Assigned Early

Once allocated, most newbies hesitate. And their strategy can be devastating with the decisions they make during that time. It's always better to know that if you trade shares, you may be given a chance. Especially if you have a multi-leg plan where you work with both long and short spreads, this can happen.

You run a long call spread and are given, for example, the higher strike short option. Many rookies and even intermediate traders are going to panic and try to get out of the situation by using the right to supply the stock for a long time. But in the long run, you're not going to make the best decision.

In this case, the best thing you can do is to sell the long option to the open market. This will allow you to catch the premium as well as the value of the product. Then you can use it to purchase the underlying stock. Once you have the stock, at the higher strike price, you will sell the stock to the option holder. This will have no impact on your plan. It will actually push you to take steps to make sure you get out of any trade with a return.

One of those times on the planet that seem unfair is being given and that world plays a game with you. You're not going to have any explanation why it happened. It just happens, and in the best way you have to live with it. If a dividend is pending, the best thing you can do to stop being allocated is to practice the call early. But both of us know it's not that easy.

As I said, the best defense against early allocation is to include in your plan the dates of dividends and earnings before initiating a deal. Otherwise, it will drive you to make decisions you won't like in the future. You're going to ask yourself what choice to exercise early–place or call?

Holding an option means you're going to sell the stock right now and   get cash. But before you do so, would you ask yourself if you want the cash right now or at the expiry date? Many traders are going to want the currency, while others may want it later. It ensures that usually put options are executed faster than puts, unless the company pays a premium, of course.

This means that when you choose to call, the dealer is willing to spend the cash now and eager to buy the underlying stock. Yet merchants are typically more inclined to spend the cash in time later. And this is when traders made the mistake of pulling the trigger too early by less qualified shares. And they're putting time premium on the table by doing that.

HOW TO RECOVER WHEN TRADES TURN AGAINST YOU

If you make profits and win every deal, it's all good and good. All go according to your plans, and you know under your belt you have these opportunities to sell. But all of a sudden you're in a position to run away from a deal because you want to stop too much risk.

How did you get to this place? How are you healing from the loss?

Recovering is a vital process to make sure you have a straight mindset and learn from your mistakes. But before all this, you want to make sure you've got enough information to help you benefit from other failures. In this part, we're going to focus on how to rebound from your defeats and why getting a clear mind is crucial and keeping things easy, particularly when they're rough.

You're asking "how do I restore my account and lower the amount of expenses I've had?" If you start to lose trades, you start to think that you can take a drastic step to get rid of all that and get back to winning trades and getting the money you like. But that's a fatal error. You should never make any drastic changes to the way you deal, as you will lose a lot of money in the long run. You should understand that there is no plot against you on the market. You can't restore your account immediately.

That's how you slowly and steadily restore your trading account so you've learnt it all along the way and become a smarter, stronger investor.

1. STOP TRADING WITH REAL MONEY

This may sound crazy and unproductive, but right now you must stop it. This will discourage you from losing more money due to the mistakes you made in a routine. Give yourself a break and admit that you've lost a lot of money. One of the reasons why avoiding selling is recommended is because you could invest in a vengeance mentality, which is the best way to lose all the money you've got.

2. CLEAR YOUR HEAD

Use this time to clear your mind and assess the things that cost your money now that you have stopped trading. When you find out those stuff, you can understand that you really feel good because you now know that you can close the door.

Losses would lead to a psychological thing for some people. If you're one of those, so before you get back to trading, you want to make sure you get back into the right mindset. When dealing, you would like to be relaxed and constructive. Yet stop being over-confident and pessimistic as this results in defeats.

3. DEMO TRADING

Now that you've learned the things that lead to defeats, you can test different demo account techniques and ideas to make sure they're working in real life. Use this time to really nail it down and know exactly what steps to take to come out with a profit and win nearly every trade in different situations. It's like a day of work. And make sure you're going through these hours and enjoy doing it because this will save you from wasting thousands of dollars in real-life trades.

Test trading will also help you get into the right mindset, as when you start winning trades in your test accounts, you can increase your confidence in live trading. Once you see that in your demo account you're doing exceptionally well and you've corrected your errors, it's time to get back to regular trading.

4. START LIVE TRADING

Now you know how to handle different situations and how to handle things. This is the time to remember you've been putting in the hours and you've become a better trader because of earlier losses. Always allow your past experiences to determine your acts in live trading. And if you catch yourself making the same faults, then repeat steps 2 so 3 to get to the right side again.

Also, even for the best of us, this happens. This is a common thing and you shouldn't be afraid to admit that you're taking some time off dealing because you're not in the right mindset. A professional trader can realize that your attitude has a lot to do with how you get out of any market.

5. MAINTAIN RISK DISCIPLINE

When you're live trading, there will be moments if you think it's going to be worth taking a huge gamble. But then you realize it wasn't, and the loss will make you rattled. You should know that it is not your net worth, but self-worth.

You should be able to deal confidently with the defeats. Your attitude plays a very important role in the way your next trade is going to go, as stated before. You can either let gods trading decide where you're going to end up, or you can take responsibility and pave your own path.

Once you learn to deal positively with the losses, you become a professional trader immediately. If they lose, novice traders get angry, and that anger takes their best. Professional traders are disciplining themselves and telling themselves that this often occurs, and it is their decision if they lose the next exchange because of it or win it and rebound from the defeat.

Ultimately, by doubling in the markets, you should never try to compensate for previous defeats.

You're going to find yourself in that position many times as a novice. You're going to be motivated to keep selling the same alternative you started with and try to double it if you win it. You begin to think the whole world is false and you only know what's going on around.

CONCLUSION

As mentioned in the beginning of this book, for thousands of years, options' trading has been in use in some way. All the ideas you've heard about successful options trading here are confined to stocks. The CBOE and other markets have platforms for a variety of other instruments such as currencies, exchange traded funds, mutual funds, derivatives, stocks, and more to buy and sell options. If you already have a fair level of industry experience in any of these fields, then you can extend your knowledge to trade options.

Just try to remember these four points to survive the investment world:

Get Permission: mind, you must always get your broker's permission to start trading options. This is the rule of the SEC! If approval is granted, it means that your financial situation is in line with options trading requirements. It is most likely that new traders will only be licensed for simple option strategies.

Practice: You can also choose "paper deal" options, as with trading stocks. This will teach you risk-free information and allow you to join the "real world" of trading options. Practice until the simple techniques are familiar with you.

Be disciplined: keep your portfolio products up-to-date and follow YOUR guidelines for each transaction you have made. For starters, if you enter a trade with the intention of not keeping it for more than a month then stick to your guns and continue in that direction.

Keep track of the expiry dates: Knowing the expiry date is essential to manage the position of an option. At first, if you're only concerned with a trade or two, it may not be too hard, but once you get big, you'll need to design a system to keep track of each expiry date.

What we hopefully achieved by writing this book is a summary-level description of the essential options trading mechanics. Beyond the world of spreads, strangles, and straddles, there are a number of (and more complex) options available to trading strategies.